SCHOLASTIC

Teaching With Favorite
Jan Brett
Books

BY JACQUELINE CLARKE

NEW YORK • TORONTO • LONDON • AUCKLAND • SYDNEY
MEXICO CITY • NEW DELHI • HONG KONG • BUENOS AIRES

Teaching
Resources

Edited by Joan Novelli
Cover and interior design by Kathy Massaro
Interior illustrations by Maxie Chambliss

ISBN: 0-439-39509-7
Copyright © 2005 by Jacqueline Clarke.
All rights reserved.
Printed in the U.S.A.
Published by Scholastic Inc.

8 9 10   40   12

Contents

About This Book

With each new book, Jan Brett creates a miniature world for children to explore. Her "more is more" approach to illustration begs readers to revisit her books again and again—each time finding something new to delight their senses. Hidden in the borders or side panels of each story is a second story just waiting to be discovered.

Jan Brett's books are full of surprises, yet at the same time they establish a sense of intimacy with readers. All reflect her love of animals and nature. Many are set in places she has visited and include people she knows. Even her beloved pets are central figures in many of her stories. Through her work she has found a way to communicate with children by blending her everyday world with the one in which she dreams.

As you share Jan Brett's books with children, use this resource as a guide for exploring the different facets of her work. Many of the activities are drawn from "behind the scenes" information about how the characters, setting, plot, and even title came to be. Here's a look at what you'll find:

◎ **About Jan Brett:** "What did Jan Brett want to be when she was a child? What were her favorite things to do?" Use the information on page 5 to answer these and other questions about this favorite author.

◎ **Before Reading:** Suggestions for introducing each of 12 featured books help activate prior knowledge and teach prediction skills.

◎ **After Reading:** This section includes discussion starters for each book that target specific reading skills, plus activities for extending learning, including vocabulary-building ideas, hands-on math lessons, poetry, interactive displays, class books, and science investigations.

◎ **Reproducible Activity Pages:** These ready-to-use pages support teaching with each featured book and encourage independent learning with mini-books, games, writing frames, and more.

◎ **Teaching With Other Favorite Jan Brett Books:** For additional titles written and/or illustrated by Jan Brett, and suggestions for teaching with them, see pages 61–64.

Tip
▲▲▲▲▲

Planning an Author-Illustrator Study

If you plan on reading several books by Jan Brett, you might want to conduct an author-illustrator study. Suggestions for doing so are on pages 6 and 7.

Meet the Author-Illustrator

Jan Brett was a shy child who spent much of her time drawing and daydreaming. The pictures she drew became a way of expressing herself. Reading was also a favorite pleasure. "I remember the special quiet of rainy days when I felt that I could enter the pages of my beautiful picture books," she says (from Authors Online; **www.scholastic.com**). One of her favorite books was *Millions and Millions of Cats*, by Wanda Gag. Inspired by the story, she would imagine that her backyard was filled with cats and she'd picture each one. By the time she was six years old, she'd woven her love of books and drawing into her dreams for the future. "If you had gone to my kindergarten class and asked me what I wanted to be, I'd have said, 'a children's book illustrator.' That's all I've ever wanted to be" (from *Meet the Authors and Illustrators: Volume Two,* by Deborah Kovacs and James Preller; Scholastic, 1993).

In 1970, she attended the Boston Museum of Fine Arts, where she refined her artistic abilities. She began her career in children's literature as an illustrator of books such as St. *Patrick's Day in the Morning*, by Eve Bunting (Clarion, 1980). At the urging of an editor, she wrote and illustrated her first book, *Fritz and the Beautiful Horses* (Houghton Mifflin) in 1981.

Today she lives in Norwell, Massachusetts, with her husband, Joe, a bass player with the Boston Symphony Orchestra. When she's not creating picture books, she enjoys horseback riding, reading, baking, knitting, and needlepoint. She also likes to travel and visits many of the places that become the settings for her books. "From cave paintings to Norwegian sleighs to Japanese gardens, I study the traditions of many countries I visit and use them as a starting point for my children's books" (from About Jan Brett; **www.janbrett.com**).

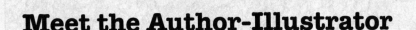

Connections to the Language Arts Standards

The activities found in this book will support you in meeting the following standards as outlined by Mid-Continent Regional Educational Laboratory (MCREL), an organization that collects and synthesizes national and state K–12 standards:

Reading:
◆ Uses the general skills and strategies of the reading process
◆ Uses reading skills and strategies to understand and interpret a variety of literary texts

Writing:
◆ Uses the general skills and strategies of the writing process
◆ Uses the stylistic and rhetorical aspects of writing
◆ Uses grammatical and mechanical conventions in written composition
◆ Gathers and uses information for research purposes

Listening and Speaking:
◆ Uses listening and speaking strategies for different purposes

Source: *Content Knowledge: A Compendium of Standards and Benchmarks for K–12 Education* (4th ed.). Mid-Continent Research for Education and Learning, 2004.

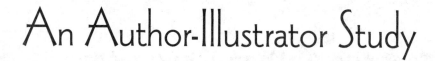

An Author-Illustrator Study

Help students make deeper connections between the books, the author-illustrator, and themselves by planning a Jan Brett author-illustrator study. By comparing characters, settings, illustrations, themes, and so on, students begin to understand the authoring and illustrating process as well as learn how books "work."

Author Center

Set up a display area to use throughout your study. Include some or all of the following:

◎ books written, retold, and illustrated by the author-illustrator

◎ clippings of interviews or articles

◎ photos

◎ contact information (see Additional Resources, page 7)

◎ student projects based on the books

◎ copies of related masks, puppets, cards, and clip art (available at the Jan Brett Web site; see Additional Resources, page 7)

◎ book review forms

Introduce the Author

Of all her books, Jan Brett considers *Trouble With Trolls* to be most representative of her style. "It has snow, animals, a hedgehog story, and best of all, the hero is a little girl," she says (from Authors Online; **www.scholastic.com**). Use this book to introduce Jan Brett. Share with students that, like many authors, she writes about what she knows and loves. Throughout the author-illustrator study, challenge students to look for these same elements in her other books. You may want to create a chart to record the information and help students make comparisons.

Create a Time Line

Examine Jan Brett's career as an author-illustrator by creating a time line of her work.

◎ Collect as many books by Jan Brett as possible. (See Additional Resources, page 7, for information.) As you read each one, place the book on the chalkboard tray. Sequence the books by copyright date to create a time line of titles.

◎ Gather students around the time line. Ask: "What does Jan Brett's work tell you about her as a person? As a writer? As an illustrator? How has her work changed over the years? What elements do you think her books share? How would you describe her style?" Encourage students to give reasons for their responses.

Book Tour

Many of Jan Brett's books are set in places children have never visited, such as Norway (*Trouble With Trolls*), Switzerland (*Gingerbread Baby*), and China (*Daisy Comes Home*).

As you read her books, mark the setting of each story on a world map. Explain that the author traveled to many, if not all, of these places to take photographs and gather information that she would later use in her stories and pictures. At the end of the study, gather children around the map. Ask the following:

◎ "Where does Jan Brett live?" (*Norwell, Massachusetts*) Mark this on the map.

◎ "Which setting in her books is farthest from her home? Closest to her home?"

◎ "Which setting in her books is farthest from your home? Closest to your home?"

◎ "How many books were set in Europe? North America?" (Continue with other continents.)

◎ "Where would you like the setting of her next book to be?"

Border Art

Jan Brett's signature style is characterized by colorful story borders. She uses these to capture her "overflow thoughts." *Annie and the Wild Animals* was the first book in which she used this technique.

Gather books by Jan Brett that use borders or story panels. Work together with students to examine each one and identify the purpose of the borders or panels in each book—for example, to tell a second story or to foreshadow.

Read aloud the story *Little Red Riding Hood*. Let students illustrate a page from the story, using borders or panels. They can do this by showing the wolf going to Grandma's house in the main picture while Little Red Riding Hood is picking flowers in the borders. Encourage creativity by focusing on detail in the drawings.

Fascination Boxes

Jan Brett, like many authors, writes about the things that fascinate her, including hens, hedgehogs, and trolls. Ask students to fill a shoe box with pictures of things or objects that fascinate them. Let them take turns sharing the items with classmates. Encourage them to use their fascination boxes for inspiration in their writing.

Additional Resources

Books

The Author Studies Handbook
by Laura Kotch
(Scholastic, 1995).

This resource offers numerous ideas for launching and carrying out an author study. Includes photos and samples of student work.

The Big Book of Picture-Book Authors & Illustrators
by James Preller
(Scholastic, 2001).

Jan Brett is included in this book of 60 profiles of authors and illustrators. Also available, *Meet the Authors and Illustrators: Volume One* (Scholastic, 1991).

Web Site

The Official Jan Brett Web Site
(www.janbrett.com)

Visit Jan Brett's Web site to find book-related activities and printouts including masks, puppets, and props. Educators can also request a teacher's pack, which includes "newsnotes" on many of her books. An e-mail option allows students to write to the author-illustrator to suggest book ideas, ask questions, or tell about their own writing or drawing.

Fritz and the Beautiful Horses

(HOUGHTON MIFFLIN, 1981)

Concepts and Themes

▲▲▲▲▲▲

* horses
* diversity/tolerance
* character
* heroism
* perspective

The citizens do not let Fritz into the walled city because they do not consider him beautiful. Yet he is gentle, kind, surefooted, and hard working. Through an act of bravery and heroism, he proves that there is more to him than meets the eye.

Before Reading

Beautiful Is...

Introduce the story with a quick-write in which students define what they think *beautiful* means. Together, look up the word in a dictionary. Let students compare their definitions with the dictionary definition.

Mini-Dictionary

Create a mini-dictionary to familiarize children with the horse-related vocabulary used in the book. Review the words.

◎ Give each child a copy of the mini-dictionary (page 11), and review the words.

◎ Invite students to name other words that relate to horses—for example, *stable* and *saddle*. After reading the story, students can choose a new word about horses to add to page six of their dictionaries. Have them draw and label a picture and write a definition.

◎ Have students color and cut out the pages, then staple them together in alphabetical order. Read the book together.

After Reading

Use the story to further explore the concept of beautiful and to make connections to character, theme, and point of view.

◉ Ask students to decide whether they think Fritz is beautiful based on their definition of the word (see Before Reading, "Beautiful Is...").

◉ Write the following sentence starters on the chalkboard and have students choose one to complete:

Fritz is beautiful because _____ .

Fritz is not beautiful because _____ .

◉ Discuss Fritz's character as it relates to the theme of the story. Ask: "How has reading the story changed your point of view? What would you add to or remove from your definition of beautiful? Can your definition and someone else's both be right?"

Extension Activities

Beauty Boxes (Social Studies and Language Arts)

Use this lesson to reinforce the use of adjectives and to explore the idea that beauty can be found inside and out.

◉ Elicit adjectives from students that describe Fritz, such as *gentle*, *kind*, and *surefooted*. Write each word on a slip of paper.

◉ Place the words in a box covered with plain brown paper and show it to students. Explain that although this package may not be wrapped beautifully on the outside, it's what's inside that **really** counts. Unwrap the package and read the adjectives aloud.

◉ Give each student a box. Invite students to write adjectives that describe them on the "inside" (such as *kind* and *curious*). Let students decorate their boxes—for example, with a picture of themselves. Encourage children to "look inside" to get to know their classmates and friends better.

Book Links

A Field Full of Horses
by Peter Hansard
(Candlewick Press, 1993).

Join the author in a "field full of horses" as he describes in first-person narrative what he loves about these animals. Also included are facts and diagrams that teach children about a horse's anatomy, color, size, and more.

Five O'Clock Charlie
by Marguerite Henry
(Aladdin, 1995).

Poor old Charlie! Mr. Spinks has retired him to a small field, and he misses his days as a workhorse. Discover how Charlie finds himself a new job and feels important once again.

My Pony Book
by Louise Pritchard
(DK Publishing, 1998).

Each two-page spread features photographs, diagrams, and short paragraphs that teach children how to care for a pony.

Hands-On Measuring (Math)

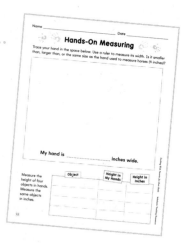

A horse's height is measured by the width of a human hand, with the standard being 4 inches, or 10 centimeters. Use this information as the basis for exploring nonstandard and standard measurement.

◎ Share the following information about measurements for a pony and a horse:

> pony: fewer than 14.2 hands
> horse: 14.2 hands or more

◎ Give each child a copy of the record sheet (page 12).

◎ Guide students in tracing and measuring their own hand, as well as using their hand and a ruler to measure objects in the classroom.

◎ Follow up by letting students share measurements taken with their hands and those taken with rulers. How do they compare? Use results to lead a discussion about the value of standard measurement.

Word Study: Giddyup! (Language Arts and Movement)

How many verbs can students name that tell how horses move? Use this lively activity to explore this part of speech.

◎ Share examples from the book, such as *gallop*, *prance*, *leap*, and *buck*.

◎ Encourage students to name others, such as *trot* and *canter*. List them on a chart.

◎ Work together with students to define each verb. Let students take turns choosing one to act out while the class guesses what it is.

muzzle: the nose and jaws of a horse

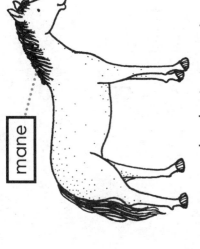

mane: the hair growing from the head and neck of a horse

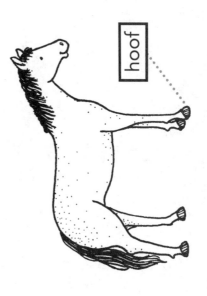

hoof: the hard covering over a horse's foot

My Horse Dictionary

Name _____

coat: the outer covering of a horse

Teaching With Favorite Jan Brett Books   Scholastic Teaching Resources

Hands-On Measuring

Trace your hand in the space below. Use a ruler to measure its width. Is it smaller than, larger than, or the same size as the hand used to measure horses (4 inches)?

My hand is _____ **inches wide.**

	Object	Height in My Hands	Height in Inches
Measure the height of four objects in hands. Measure the same objects in inches.			

Teaching With Favorite Jan Brett Books   Scholastic Teaching Resources

Annie and the Wild Animals

(HOUGHTON MIFFLIN, 1985)

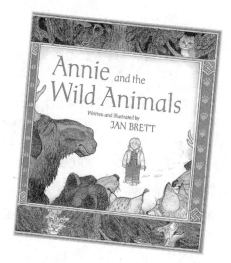

When Annie's cat disappears, she hopes to find a new pet by leaving corn cakes at the edge of the wood. Her plan works, but none of the animals are quite what she expected. Just when she thinks she'll never find a new pet, Taffy reappears joined by many small, furry friends.

Concepts and Themes

- ☼ animals
- ☼ winter
- ☼ pets
- ☼ problem solving

Before Reading

Pet Detectives

Introduce the story with a sorting exercise that encourages students to answer the question, "What makes a good pet?" Gather several pictures of animals. If possible, include the animals from the book. Divide the class into small groups. Give each group a set of pictures. Ask students to sort the animals into two groups: "makes a good pet" and "doesn't make a good pet." Let groups take turns naming the animals in each category. Discuss why some animals make good pets while others do not. Introduce the terms *wild* and *domesticated*.

After Reading

Use the story to explore character development and to examine the degree to which a character changes as a result of his or her experiences.

- ◎ How did Annie feel at the beginning of the book?
- ◎ How did Annie feel at the end of the book?
- ◎ What caused her feelings to change?
- ◎ Has this story changed you in any way?

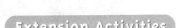

Sometimes I Feel Lonely (Social Studies and Language Arts)

Throughout much of the story, Annie feels lonely. Take time to explore this emotion with children.

◎ Write "lonely" on the chalkboard. Discuss its meaning.

◎ Guide students to discover the words *lone* and *one* inside the word *lonely*. Ask: "How do these words relate to its meaning?"

◎ Show students the cover of the book. Ask them to decide whether they think Annie is feeling lonely in this picture.

◎ Ask children to share reasons someone might feel lonely—for example, a new student might feel lonely until he or she makes a new friend or feels more comfortable in a new classroom. Students might like to role-play some of these situations in small groups. This will help them understand that everyone feels like this at one time or another and also provide opportunities to practice age-appropriate responses when such situations arise in students' own lives.

"Missing" and "Wanted" Posters

(Language Arts and Art)

Encourage students to identify with Annie's problem and take action by creating "Wanted" and "Missing" posters. First they must extract details and organize pertinent information.

◎ Ask students what strategies Annie used to find Taffy and search for a new pet. Invite children to share other strategies she might have tried.

◎ Gather several classified ads from your local newspaper. Copy them onto transparencies, and share them with children. Help them take note of the information contained in each, such as descriptions of what is wanted or missing and contact information.

◎ Let students create Missing or Wanted posters for Annie to use in her search.

◎ Display the posters on a bulletin board or in the hallway under a heading such as "We're Here to Help, Annie!"

DO Feed the Animals! (Science)

While many animals hibernate or migrate during the winter, there are also some (like those in the book) that stay active and must adapt to the change of season. Help students care for those animals by creating bird feeders.

◎ Annie's plan to find a new pet included leaving food for it to eat. Ask children if her plan would have worked as well if the story had taken place in summer. Why not?

◎ Stock a work table with sliced bread, cookie cutters, craft sticks, peanut butter, birdseed, string or yarn, and scissors.

◎ Have children cut shapes from the bread, poke a hole at the top, and let them dry overnight.

◎ The next day, have them use craft sticks to spread peanut butter on the bread and then sprinkle with birdseed.

◎ Help children loop the string through the hole and tie it at the top.

◎ Hang the bird feeders around the schoolyard, or wrap them in aluminum foil for safe transport home. If the feeders are visible from a classroom window, provide a journal for students to record observations. If children take their feeders home, periodically invite them to share observations at the morning meeting or another group time.

Tip

Learn more about pet care at these Web sites:

Pet Place
www.petplace.com

Pets for Kids
www.petsforkids.co.uk

Emma's Pet
by David McPhail
(Dutton, 1988).

Emma is searching for a pet, but none are as soft and cuddly as she would like. In the end, she finds the perfect "pet" right in her very own home.

I Want a Pet
by Lauren Child
(Tricycle Press, 1999).

Longing for a pet, the child in this story suggests many to her family members, who, for one reason or another, dismiss each as "unsuitable." The "pet shop lady" comes to the rescue with the perfect pet to meet her family's criteria.

A Pet or Not?
by Alvin Silverstein
(Twenty-First Century Books, 1999).

This book provides information about unusual pets such as armadillos, hedgehogs, monkeys, and even potbellied pigs. The last chapter, entitled "Not a Pet!," suggests that most of the animals included in the book are better off left in the wild because keeping them as pets would be quite a challenge.

Word Study: Too Big! Too Mean! Too Grumpy!

(Language Arts)

By leaving corn cakes at the edge of the wood, Annie attracts five animals that would not make good pets. She decides that the moose is too big, the wildcat is too mean, and the bear is too grumpy. Use this activity to help students identify adjectives from the story and then use them to describe various animals.

◎ Revisit the book to find the adjectives used to describe the moose, wildcat, and bear.

◎ How do you think Annie would describe the stag and the gray wolf?

> The stag is too _____ .
> The gray wolf is too _____ .

◎ Extend this lesson by using the pattern found in the book *Dear Zoo*, by Rod Campbell (Little Simon, 1999), to describe other animals:

> I wrote to the zoo to send me a pet.
> They sent me a _____ ,
> but it was too _____ !

Rhyme Time (Language Arts, Social Studies, and Health)

Many children love to pet animals. Use the following poem as a springboard for a discussion on animal safety.

Who to Pet and Who Not To

Go pet a kitten, pet a dog,
Go pet a worm for practice,
But don't go pet a porcupine—
You want to be a cactus?

—by X. J. Kennedy

Follow up by asking children: "Why does the poet tell us not to pet a porcupine? Which other animals might be difficult to pet?" Discuss reasons that children should not pet some animals, including cats and dogs they don't know. Let children share rules their families have about animals—for example, "Don't pet an animal you don't know" or "Ask for permission before you pet an animal."

Goldilocks and the Three Bears

❖

(PUTNAM, 1987)

This traditional retelling of a favorite tale is accompanied by lavish illustrations that include beautifully detailed costumes and intricately carved furnishings that adorn the bears' home.

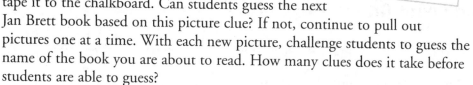

Before Reading

Guessing Game

Before introducing this book, play a guessing game that builds critical-thinking skills. Color and cut out the pictures of bears, bowls, chairs, and beds (page 20). Place them in a paper bag. Pull out a picture and tape it to the chalkboard. Can students guess the next Jan Brett book based on this picture clue? If not, continue to pull out pictures one at a time. With each new picture, challenge students to guess the name of the book you are about to read. How many clues does it take before students are able to guess?

The Rule of Three

Once students have guessed the story, use the picture clues to teach students about the "rule of three."

◎ Ask a volunteer to sort the pictures into categories, such as "bears," "bowls," "chairs," and "beds." Ask: "How many objects are in each category?"

◎ Explain that this folktale uses the rule of three as part of its story structure. It includes three bear characters and three story events with three objects in each. (Goldilocks finds three bowls, three chairs, and three beds.)

◎ Can students name other stories that utilize the rule of three? (Examples include *The Three Little Pigs*, by Steven Kellogg, HarperCollins, 2002; *The Three Questions*, by Jon Muth, Scholastic, 2002; and *The Three Sillies*, by Paul Galdone, Clarion, 1981.)

Concepts and Themes

▲▲▲▲▲

☼ folktales

☼ size relationships

☼ conventions of storytelling (the "rule of three")

Tip

▲▲▲▲▲

Children can use the pictures on page 20 as props for retelling the story. To make puppets, have children glue or tape each picture to a craft stick.

Use this story to help students make inferences based on what they already know about Goldilocks and her experiences.

◎ Revisit the last page of the book. (It shows Goldilocks running away.) Reread the sentence, "And what happened to Goldilocks, no one can tell."

◎ Ask students to spend a few minutes thinking about Goldilocks and what she might do next.

◎ Have students draw a picture and write (or dictate) a few sentences about what they think happened to Goldilocks after she left the bears' house.

◎ Follow up by reading aloud *Goldilocks Returns*, by Lisa Campbell Ernst (Simon & Schuster, 2000). This sequel tells the story of a middle-aged Goldilocks (now called Goldie) who currently owns a lock shop and returns to the bears' home to make amends and ease her guilty conscience.

◎ Let children compare this sequel to their own ideas about Goldilocks's future. What are the similarities? What are the differences?

Extension Activities

You Can Count On the Three Bears! (Math and Language Arts)

Use *Goldilocks and the Three Bears* as a springboard for some creative counting.

◎ Copy the three-bears number line and bear counters (page 21). Cut apart the number line segments and tape together as indicated.

◎ Make multiple copies of each bear pattern. Cut out a dozen or so Baby Bear counters and number them 3, 6, 9, 12, and so on (to skip-count by threes, starting with three).

◎ Once children are familiar with counting by threes from three, challenge them to count by threes using Mama Bear. Number the Mama Bear counters according to a new counting pattern, such as 2, 5, 8, 11, and so on. Repeat with Papa Bear and a new counting pattern.

Pass the Bear (Language Arts)

Retelling stories gives children a sense of how stories "work." Play this game to retell the story of the three bears.

◎ Gather children in a circle. While holding a stuffed bear, say, "Once upon a time there were three bears."

◎ Pass the bear to a student and invite him or her to add on to the story with one sentence.

◎ Continue playing, giving a different child a turn each time, until the story reaches its end.

New and Improved (Science)

Can students use their problem-solving skills to build a chair strong enough to hold Goldilocks?

◎ Divide the class into small groups. Ask each group to design and build a chair strong enough to hold Goldilocks. Provide simple materials such as tongue depressors, interlocking blocks, clay, and cardboard.

◎ Let groups test their designs by placing a small doll (representing Goldilocks) in the chair. If it doesn't break, they have successfully met the challenge!

Word Study: Big, Bigger, Biggest! (Language Arts and Math)

Take advantage of the size relationships found in *Goldilocks and the Three Bears* to teach about comparative language.

◎ Color and cut out the pictures of the bears (page 20) and display them for students. Brainstorm comparative language (such as *big*, *bigger*, *biggest*) to describe the bears. Record the words on a chart. Repeat the process for the bowls, chairs, and beds.

◎ Give each student a sheet of 8- by 11-inch paper. Show students how to fold the paper in half the long way and cut the top flap into thirds.

◎ Ask children to choose one set of comparative terms (for example, *long*, *longer*, *longest*) and write one on each flap.

◎ Under each flap, have children draw the corresponding picture from the story.

◎ Let students take turns sharing their flap books with classmates.

Guessing Game

Teaching With Favorite Jan Brett Books   Scholastic Teaching Resources

A

0   1   2   3   4   5   6   7   8

Tape A here.

B

9   10   11   12   13   14   15   16   17

Tape B here.

18   19   20   21   22   23   24   25

You Can Count On the Three Bears!

21

The Mitten

(G.P. PUTNAM'S SONS, 1989)

Concepts and Themes

- animals
- winter
- habitats

At Nikki's request, Baba knits him a pair of white mittens. "If you drop one in the snow," she warns, "you'll never find it." As she predicts, Nikki loses a mitten while wandering through the wintry countryside. It's found by a series of woodland animals who, one by one, crawl inside the snug mitten. At the end of the story, a bear's big "achoo" sends the animals soaring in all directions. Nikki eventually finds his mitten and is left wondering why it is stretched out and larger than its mate.

Before Reading

I Spy a Mitten

Share the cover of the book with students. Let them name each animal. Ask: "What are the animals looking at?" (*a mitten*) Invite students to make predictions about what the animals are thinking as they gaze at the mitten. Students can do this orally or write the words in "thought bubbles" for each animal.

Lost and Found Stories

Develop prewriting skills and an understanding of story structure by asking students to imagine they're the authors of this story.

- Ask: "In your story, how does the mitten end up in the woods?" Discuss students' suggested story lines. Then reveal that a young boy named Nikki lost it while playing in the snow.

- Invite students to share stories about things they have lost (and hopefully found).

After Reading

By not writing text for the last page of the book, the author invites readers to draw their own conclusions about what Baba might be thinking or saying.

◎ Revisit the last page of *The Mitten*. It shows Baba wearing a perplexed look as she holds the stretched-out mitten.

◎ Give students time to study the picture. Ask: "What is Baba thinking? What might she say?"

◎ Invite children to write their own text for the page and share it with classmates.

Extension Activities

How Do You Say *Grandma?* (Language Arts and Social Studies)

Build vocabulary by exploring different words people use for *grandmother*.

◎ Ask students to remember what Nikki called his grandmother. (*Baba*) Explain that this is what grandmothers are often called in the Ukraine, where the story takes place.

◎ Challenge students to find out what children in other countries call their grandmothers. For example, in Spain a grandmother is called *abuela* and in France, *grande-mère*.

◎ List these on a chart along with nicknames students have for their own grandmothers—for example, *nana* or *grams*.

◎ Use these names to fill in the squares of a blank bingo board. Play the game as you would a regular game of bingo, but let the winner call out "grandmother" using the language or nickname of his or her choice.

Ya Ya	Grandmother	Bube	Grams	Mimi
Grammy	Big Mama	Nanny	Oma	Litta
Lela	Grandma	FREE	Gigi	Baba
Nai Nai	Vovo	Moggy	Nanny	Ajji
Nonna	Gam	grande-mère	Granny	Mams

How Big Is Your Mitten? (Math)

The mitten in the story is stretched to a size large enough to hold a mole, rabbit, hedgehog, owl, badger, fox, bear, and mouse. Invite students to measure and compare the size of their own mittens.

◎ Ask each student to bring a mitten to school. Have extras on hand for students to use as needed.

◎ Have students trace their mitten on a sheet of paper.

◎ Then have children use a ruler to measure and record the length and width of their mitten.

◎ To measure volume, first have students fill their mitten to capacity using pieces of foam packing material. Next, have them remove the pieces, count them, and write the total number on the paper.

◎ Help students compare their mittens. How many of their mittens put together do students think it would take to hold all the animals from the story?

The Mitten Tree (Social Studies and Math)

Nikki had a pair of warm mittens to protect him from the cold. Involve students in a community service project to benefit those not as fortunate as Nikki.

◎ Introduce the project by reading aloud *The Mitten Tree*, by Candace Christiansen (Fulcrum, 1997). This book tells the story of an elderly woman who secretly knits mittens and hangs them on a tree for the children waiting at the bus stop.

◎ Help children create and distribute flyers asking families to donate mittens to children who need them. Include the dates of the project and drop-off location(s).

◎ Set up a tree (real or artificial) in the classroom or school lobby. As mittens are received, let children hang them on the tree with clothespins.

◎ Integrate math into the project by letting students count and sort the mittens collected.

◎ At the end of the drive, distribute the mittens to local charities or school nurses in various districts.

Tip
▲▲▲▲▲▲

As a variation on the service-project theme of this activity, invite children to collect mittens to share with children at school who have forgotten theirs.

Animal Research Riddles (Science and Language Arts)

The story shows animals seeking shelter inside a lost mitten. How do animals really find shelter during the winter months? Work with children to collect and share information in the form of riddles.

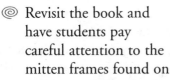
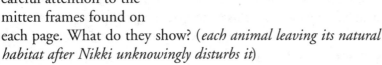

◎ Revisit the book and have students pay careful attention to the mitten frames found on each page. What do they show? (*each animal leaving its natural habitat after Nikki unknowingly disturbs it*)

◎ Work together with students to list the ways each animal prepares for and survives the winter. Include information about protection, habitat, and food consumption.

◎ Give each child a sheet of drawing paper. From the information gathered, have students write three clues about one of the animals. They can illustrate a forest scene around the clues that includes a picture of the animal.

◎ On a separate sheet of paper, ask students to draw, color, and cut out a mitten shape that is large enough to cover their animal. Show students how to glue one edge of the mitten to the paper so that it covers the animal and creates a flap.

◎ Display the riddles on a hallway bulletin board for other classes to enjoy, or compile them to make a class book.

Word Study: Move Like the Animals (Language Arts)

Use this movement activity to highlight verbs from the story.

◎ Revisit the book and search for verbs that tell how the animals moved. For example, the mole *burrowed,* the owl *swooped,* the bear *lumbered,* and the mouse *wriggled.*

◎ Write these words on slips of paper and place them in a bag.

◎ Let children take turns choosing a slip and acting it out for the class to guess.

Berlioz
the Bear

(G.P. PUTNAM'S SONS, 1991)

W hile on his way to a village ball, Berlioz and his orchestra meet misfortune when the wheel of their bandwagon gets stuck in a pothole. Led by a stubborn mule that refuses to move, they enlist the help of a succession of animals. In the end it's the bee, stuck in Berlioz's string bass, that makes it possible for them to get to the ball on time.

Concepts and Themes

▲▲▲▲▲▲▲

☼ music

☼ responsibility

☼ cumulative tales

Before Reading

Getting to the Ball on Time

Introduce the story by discussing the concept of responsibility. Explain that Berlioz (pronounced BEAR-lee-oze) and his orchestra are responsible for getting to the village ball on time. Ask: "What might the consequences be if the band is late?" Ask students to share their experiences with being late to important events. Discuss ways the class works together to be on time—for example, everyone helps pick up so that students can get to lunch on time.

It Figures!

"Stubborn as a mule" and "jump on the bandwagon" are figures of speech that are significant to the story *Berlioz the Bear*. Write them on the chalkboard and discuss their meanings with children. As you read the book aloud, challenge students to discover how each relates to the story.

After Reading

Follow up reading with an examination of cumulative story structure and figures of speech as they relate to *Berlioz the Bear*.

◎ Talk with students about the similarities between this book and other cumulative tales such as *The Little Engine That Could*, by Watty Piper (Grosset & Dunlap, 1978), or *The Enormous Turnip*, by Kathy

Parkinson (Albert Whitman, 1987). Ask: "How are they the same? How are they different?" Encourage students to try out a cumulative pattern when writing their own stories.

◎ Ask students whether they think the author was influenced by the saying "stubborn as a mule" when she chose a mule to lead the wagon. Encourage them to explain why or why not. Discuss the meaning of *bandwagon* as it is used in the story. Compare this to the word's meaning in the saying. Ask: "How does the cumulative pattern of the story relate to the saying, 'jump on the bandwagon?'"

Extension Activities

Meet the Real Berlioz (Social Studies)

Jan Brett named the character of Berlioz after the French composer Hector Berlioz (from **www.janbrett.com**). Use the reproducible (page 29) to help students make a connection between the story and the life and work of the composer for whom the bear was named. Invite children to compare their life to his by filling in the blanks on the right side of the paper.

Imaginations Take Flight (Music, Art, and Language Arts)

Jan Brett was listening to the Boston Symphony Orchestra when she got the idea for Berlioz the Bear. In her own words, "Music does that. It leads one to interesting places." Invite students to get lost in their own thoughts as they listen to music.

◎ Revisit the last page of the book. Ask students, "What song is Berlioz playing?" (*"Flight of the Bumblebee," by Rimski-Korsakov*)

◎ Locate a recording of this piece and play it for students. (You might try *Ofra Harnoy, Volume 4: Flight of the Bumblebee and other Virtuoso Showpieces*, 1996.)

◎ Invite them to draw pictures while they listen, to see where the music leads them.

◎ As an extension, students can write their own stories based on ideas they get from the music.

Tip

▲▲▲▲▲▲▲

For more information about Hector Berlioz, the composer who inspired the book's character, and the four families of instruments (hear them, too), check these Web sites:

Classical Music Pages:
w3.rz-berlin.mpg.de/cmp/berlioz.html

Dallas Symphony Orchestra:
www.dsokids.com

Book Links

Meet the Orchestra
by Ann Hayes
(Harcourt Brace Jovanovich, 1995).

This book makes a great introduction to the various musical instruments that make up an orchestra.

Zin! Zin! Zin! A Violin
by Lloyd Moss
(Simon & Schuster, 1995).

This musical counting book helps children learn the number of musicians (and their instruments) that make up a solo, duet, trio, and so on—all the way up to a chamber of ten!

Meet the Instrument Families (Math and Music)

Berlioz's band was made up of six different instruments: string bass, drum, trombone, clarinet, violin, and French horn. Use this activity to help students identify each one and sort it into its instrument family.

◎ On the chalkboard, write the names of the instruments in Berlioz's band. Have students group them by instrument "families": strings, percussion, woodwinds, and brass.

◎ Explain that instruments are related by the similar ways in which they produce sound. Students can regroup the instruments if necessary. Invite students to name other instruments that are part of each family.

◎ To do more, students can try grouping instruments in other ways, such as for a trio or a quartet. (See Book Links, left, for a related book.)

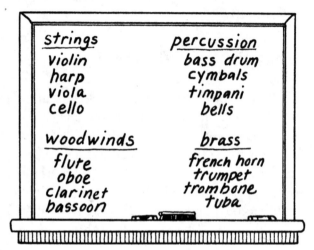

strings
violin
harp
viola
cello

percussion
bass drum
cymbals
timpani
bells

woodwinds
flute
oboe
clarinet
bassoon

brass
french horn
trumpet
trombone
tuba

Word Study: Sound Hunt (Language Arts)

Jan Brett uses words such as *buzz* and *zum* to describe sounds in her book. Explore onomatopoeia in the form of animal and musical sounds.

◎ Revisit the book to find "sound words." Challenge students to name more sound words for animals and instruments (such as *meow* and *boing*).

◎ Invite children to go on a sound hunt around the classroom or schoolyard. On a sheet of paper, ask them to record the name of the object in one column and the sound it makes in another.

◎ Have children compare their results. Did some students record different sounds for the same objects?

Name _____ Date _____

Meet the
Real Berlioz

Paste your picture here.

**All About
Hector Berlioz**

All About Me

Hector was born in 1803 in France.	I was born in _____ in _____.
As a child Hector learned how to play the flute and guitar.	I can play _____ _____.
Hector's parents convinced him to go to medical school. He was very unhappy there.	I am unhappy when _____ _____.
Hector left medical school to study his real love, music!	I love to study_____ _____.
Hector is known for his orchestral music, choral works, and operas.	My favorite kind of music is _____.

Trouble With Trolls

✦

(G.P. PUTNAM'S SONS, 1992)

Treva's troubles begin when she encounters five trolls at the top of Mount Baldy—each of whom tries to kidnap her dog, Tuffi, and keep him as a pet. But Treva is a quick thinker! She cleverly outsmarts each troll and skis to safety carrying Tuffi in her arms.

Concepts and Themes

▲▲▲▲▲▲

- ✿ trolls
- ✿ winter
- ✿ trickster tales
- ✿ problem solving

Before Reading

What's the Trouble?

Read the title of the book aloud. Can students predict the kind of trouble Treva has with the trolls? Before reading, take students on a "picture walk" through the book. Encourage them to describe what they see in the illustrations. Ask students to make a story prediction by completing this sentence:

The trouble Treva has with trolls is _____ .

Troll Profiles

The appearance and characteristics of trolls vary from story to story. Before reading the book, spend some time exploring students' perceptions of these mythical creatures.

 Give each child a sheet of paper. Have students draw a picture of a troll and complete these sentences:

Trolls are _____, _____, and _____ .
Trolls like _____ .
Trolls live _____ .

◎ Invite students to share and compare their profiles. Discuss the source of students' images of trolls—for example, are there books or movies that shaped their ideas?

Use *Trouble With Trolls* to help children explore character stereotypes and to learn how illustrations add layers to the story.

◎ Ask students to compare their troll profiles (see Before Reading) with those in the book. Ask: "How are they similar? How are they different? Have your images of trolls changed since reading the book?"

◎ Discuss ways in which characters such as trolls, giants, wolves, and princesses are sometimes stereotyped. Explore how this may add or take away from a character's development.

◎ Revisit the book and draw students' attention to the second story going on in the underground pictures. Ask: "What are the trolls doing?" (*preparing for the arrival of their new pet*) Discuss the purpose of the hedgehog in the story. (*He assumes the role set aside for the dog.*) Write the text for this "second story." Students can work together in pairs or small groups, or you can lead the class in a whole-group shared writing experience.

Extension Activities

Tricks for Trolls (Social Studies and Language Arts)

Treva used her problem-solving abilities to trick the trolls and save her dog. What would students do in the same situation?

◎ Give each student a copy of page 33. Read aloud the rhyme.

◎ Ask students to fill in the blank with the name of something they would use to trick the troll. Invite them to illustrate the words in the space provided. Let students take turns sharing their responses.

◎ Can students think of other ways to save their dog from the troll that don't involve giving him things?

Dress Like Treva (Math)

Treva's Nordic clothing is full of many beautiful patterns. Revisit the book and draw students' attention to this aspect of the illustrations.

◎ Work together to name the patterns (for example, red stripe, white stripe, red stripe, white stripe) found in her boots, socks, pants, sweater, and hat.

◎ Invite students to come to school the next day wearing as many patterns as possible. Hold a fashion show in which students take turns describing one another's patterns as they walk down the "runway."

Write a Troll Tale (Language Arts)

Inspire students to create their own "troll tales" based on troll mythology.

◎ Using books and the Internet (see Tip, left) work with students to create a list of troll folklore. For example:

> Trolls have an aversion to noise and sunlight.
> Trolls can be destroyed if a person discovers their name.
> Trolls can be warded off using mistletoe or bonfires.

◎ From the information gathered, let students choose a couple of ideas and incorporate them into an original story about a troll.

◎ Place the stories in a basket labeled "Troll Tales," and keep it in your classroom library for students to enjoy all year.

Word Study: Title Track-Down (Language Arts)

Alliteration, the repetition of the initial sounds in words, is a literary device often used in writing. *Trouble With Trolls* is an example of a book that uses alliteration in its title.

◎ Have students search through the classroom library for other titles that use alliteration. Display them on the chalkboard ledge and read each title aloud.

◎ Ask: "Why do you think authors use alliteration?"

◎ Encourage students to use this device in their own stories.

Rhyme Time (Language Arts)

You never know where a troll might be hiding! Use a poem as a springboard for creative writing.

◎ Give each student a copy of the poem (page 34). Read it aloud.

◎ Ask students to imagine that a troll is hiding in their backpack. Would they let him out? Have them complete the sentence at the bottom of the page.

◎ Then encourage them to use this sentence as a story starter for a tale about a backpack troll.

Tricks for Trolls

Name _____ Date _____

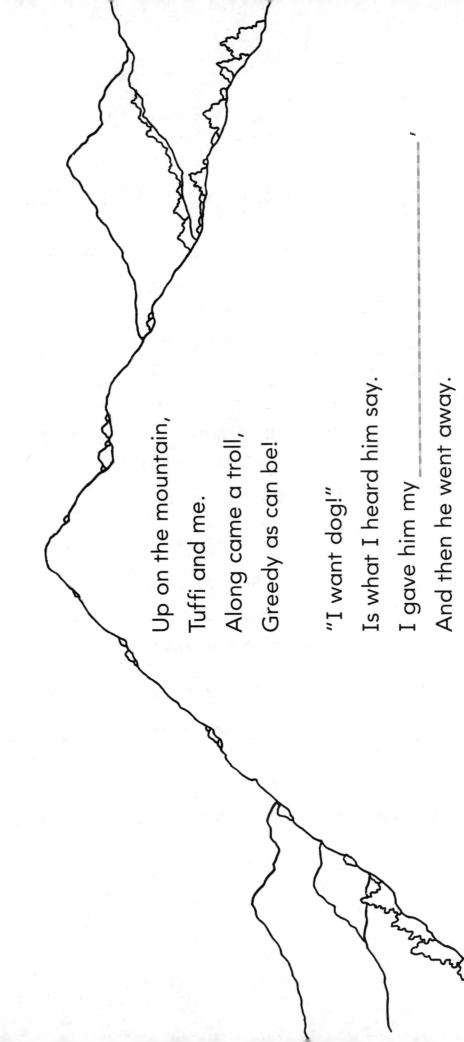

Up on the mountain,

Tuffi and me.

Along came a troll,

Greedy as can be!

"I want dog!"

Is what I heard him say.

I gave him my _____,

And then he went away.

Teaching With Favorite Jan Brett Books   Scholastic Teaching Resources

Name _____ Date _____

Backpack Trouble

You're sitting in class when
your backpack rumbles
with odd little bulges,
and mumbly grumbles—

It's all very curious,
that's certainly true.
Just don't let him out,
whatever you do!

It's definitely a troll,
What else can I say?
Keep your backpack closed—
Beware! Stowaway!

— by Kristine O'Connell George

When I found a troll in my backpack, I _____

_____

_____

_____ .

Teaching With Favorite Jan Brett Books   Scholastic Teaching Resources

Town Mouse, Country Mouse

(G.P. PUTNAM'S SONS, 1994)

Two mice couples decide to switch homes to get a taste of the "good life." Each is preyed upon by a hungry predator in their new surroundings and soon decides that "there's no place like home."

Concepts and Themes

- ☼ fables
- ☼ habitats/ environments
- ☼ food chain
- ☼ compare and contrast

Before Reading

Where Do You Live?

Before reading the book, familiarize students with the two alternating settings of the story—the town and the country. Have pictures on hand that represent town (city) life and country life. Let students sort them into two piles. Ask: "Where do you live?" Introduce the terms *rural*, *urban*, and *suburban* to further describe environments.

After Reading

Use these discussion starters to explore the theme of the story:

- ◉ Have students heard this story before? Explain that it is one of many fables originally compiled long ago by a Greek man named Aesop.

- ◉ The purpose of a fable is to teach a lesson. Ask: "What did you learn from this story?" Share the Aesop moral: "Better beans and bacon in peace than cake and ale in fear," and discuss its meaning.

- ◉ Write the following on the chalkboard: "The grass is always greener on the other side of the fence." Ask: "What is this figure of speech trying to tell us?" How does this relate to the story?

Tip

For more fables, including lesson plans for some, check this Web site:

Aesop's Fables:
www.pacific.net/~johnr/
aesop/aesop4.html;
www.umass.edu/aesop

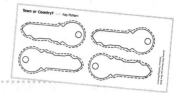

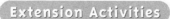

Extension Activities

Town or Country? (Math and Social Studies)

Create a graph to show students' preferences for living in a town or in the country.

◎ Make several copies of the key-shaped graph markers (page 38). On one key, write "Town" (or "City") and on the other write "Country." Use the keys to label a two-column bar graph.

◎ Give each student a key. Have students write their name on the key.

◎ Ask: "Would you rather live in a town (city) or in the country?" Let students place their key on the graph to indicate their response to the question.

◎ Discuss the results. Is there a strong preference for one type of environment over another? How do the results correspond to the environment (town, country) in which students live now? Is it the same or different? Do students agree that "the grass is greener on the other side of the fence?"

Thanks! (Language Arts)

Guests often send thank-you notes after a stay at someone's home. Invite students to write a letter from one of the mice couples to the other to say "thanks for the vacation."

◎ Give each child a blank note card. Have children write the words "Thank You" on the front and decorate as they wish.

◎ Discuss parts of a friendly letter, such as the greeting and closing. On the inside of the card, ask children to write a note telling what they liked about the visit as well as what they missed most about their own home.

◎ Give children envelopes for their cards, and let them create imaginary town or country addresses (including a return address) along with faux postage.

Predator, Prey (Science)

As important to the story as the mice are the owl and cat that try to capture them. Play a game to teach students about the dynamics between predators and prey.

◎ Have students form a large circle in an open area such as the playground or gym.

◎ Choose one child to be either the owl or cat (predator) and another to be the mouse (prey). Place a blindfold around each student's head.

◎ Invite both children to move freely inside the circle. As they do, the predator should listen carefully for sounds of the mouse and try to tag him or her. Once the mouse is caught, choose new students and repeat the game.

◎ As an extension, ask students to think about this: "Can a mouse ever be a predator? Can a cat or owl be prey?" Discuss their ideas.

Word Study: Two Sounds of C

(Language Arts)

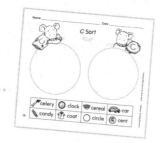

Use the words *city* and *country* to teach the two sounds of *c*.

◎ Say the two words aloud. Help students hear the difference between the hard and soft *c*.

◎ Give each student a copy of the sorting activity (page 38). Explain that the mouse with the pillow stands for the soft *c* and the mouse with the rock stands for the hard *c*.

◎ Ask students to cut out and sort the words according to their beginning letter sound (soft or hard *c*). Read the words aloud.

◎ Can students think of other words for each type of sound? Write them on the chalkboard. Let children copy them and place them in the correct group.

◎ As a challenge, add words that have each sound for *c* in the middle or end of a word (such as in *mice* or *macaroni*).

Rhyme Time (Language Arts)

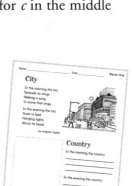

Use a poem by Langston Hughes to explore the use of personification in writing.

◎ Give each student a copy of the poem on page 39. Read it aloud together.

◎ Explain that in this poem, Langston Hughes personifies, or gives humanlike characteristics to, the city. Ask students to cite examples of this from the poem. (*"making a song," "goes to bed," "hanging lights about its head"*)

◎ Have students use the sentence starters to create their own poems that personify the country. Let students know that their poems do not have to rhyme. Students can illustrate their poems in the space provided.

◎ Invite students to share their poems with classmates. Ask: "As a person, are you more like the city or country?"

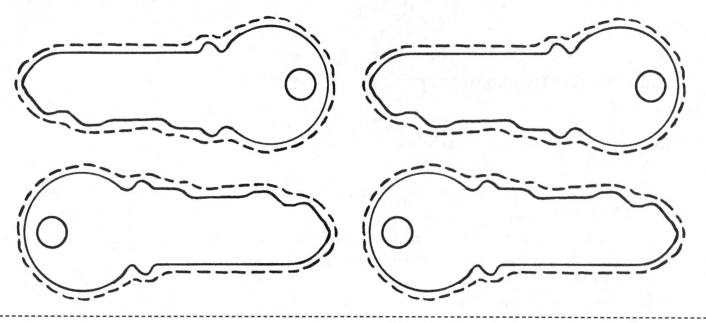

Name _____ Date _____

C Sort

◎◎

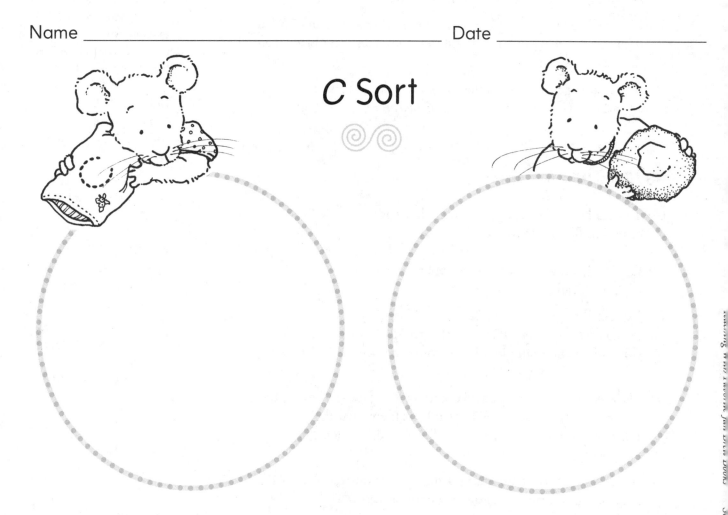

| celery | clock | cereal | car |
| candy | coat | circle | cent |

38

Name _____ Date _____

City

In the morning the city
Spreads its wings
Making a song
In stone that sings.

In the evening the city
Goes to bed
Hanging lights
About its head.

—*by Langston Hughes*

Country

In the morning the country

_____

_____

_____.

In the evening the country

_____

_____

_____.

by _____

"City" by Langston Hughes from THE LANGSTON HUGHES READER (1958). Used with permission from Harold Ober Associates.

Teaching With Favorite Jan Brett Books   Scholastic Teaching Resources

Armadillo Rodeo

(G.P. PUTNAM'S SONS, 1995)

Concepts and Themes

▲ ▲ ▲ ▲ ▲

☼ armadillos

☼ safety

☼ Texas

☼ rodeos

☼ senses

Bo is an adventuresome armadillo but he is also nearsighted—he mistakes a pair of red cowboy boots for a fellow armadillo. When he strays from his family to follow his new friend, he gets more than his share of excitement—Texas rodeo-style!

Before Reading

Dig Up Some Facts!

Armadillos are great diggers, and they especially like sandy soil. "Dig up" other facts about armadillos and share them with students before reading the book. Write each fact and the source on an armadillo-shaped cutout (page 43). Bury the facts in a tub of sand. Let students take turns digging up a fact and sharing it with the class.

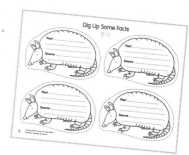

The Wanderer

Can students predict the ending after the first two pages? Show students the cover of the book. Read aloud the first two pages, stopping after "…especially Bo, who was always wandering off." Challenge students to make predictions about the rest of the story based on what they already know. Invite students to share rules they know about "wandering off." Explain that this can be very dangerous, and discuss or role-play what students can do if they find themselves separated from an adult.

After Reading

Sometimes the idea for a story comes from an interesting fact that the author discovers while researching. Use this story to explore the concepts of fact and opinion.

◎ A fact is a piece of information that is true. In this story, children learn that armadillos don't see very well. Revisit the story to highlight this piece of information. Ask: "In what ways is this fact important to the story? How would the story be different if the author hadn't included this information in the book?" Guide students in finding other facts in the story.

- An opinion reflects an individual's view. Ask: "What do you think the author thinks of armadillos? What is your opinion of armadillos? The story? Texas?"

- Make connections to other stories. Ask: "How did the author use facts in other stories? How do those stories compare to this one?"

- Go further by exploring the use of facts in nonfiction. Ask: "How does this compare with the way an author uses facts in fiction?"

Extension Activities

T Is for Texas (Social Studies and Language Arts)

Armadillo Rodeo is set in Texas, where many armadillos live. Learn more about Texas. Locate Texas on a map. If students live in another state, discuss geographic proximity—for example, how many states would students pass through to get to Texas? Is their state in the same region? Share *T Is for Texas*, by Anne Bustard (Voyageur Press, 1989), to learn more about Texas. As an extension, have students investigate what is special about the state in which they live. Using the format of *T Is for Texas* as a model, have students each choose a letter to create an alphabet book featuring their state.

Rodeo Feely Box (Science)

Since armadillos can't see very well, they rely heavily on other senses, which are usually heightened. Let students experience this concept by using a feely box.

- Show students the page in the book where Bo discovered that the boot was not an armadillo. Ask: "Which senses did he use to discover this?" (*sense of smell, touch, and sight*)

- Gather objects that might be found at a rodeo, such as a rope, cowboy hat, or even a pepper.

- Create a feely box by cutting a hole in a covered box (big enough for a child's arm to fit through).

- Place the objects in the box (one at a time). Let students take turns feeling each object and shaking the box. How many objects can they identify without their sense of sight?

Tip

▲▲▲▲▲▲

Learn more about armadillos with these Web sites:

The Mammals of Texas:
www.nsrl.ttu.edu/tmotl/
dasynove.htm

Texas Parks and Wildlife:
www.tpwd.state.tx.us/nature/
wild/mammals/dillo.htm

Book Links

Armadillo Ray
by John Beifuss
(Chronicle, 1995).

When a young armadillo is puzzled about how the moon changes shape and disappears, he decides to ask other desert dwellers. Each response is more magical than the next but hardly seems believable. Finally, the owl tells him the truth about the moon, which he discovers is the most amazing story of all.

Armadillo Tattletale
by Helen Ketteman
(Scholastic, 2000).

With ears as tall as a jackrabbit's, Armadillo often uses them for eavesdropping. But each time he repeats something that "wasn't meant for his ears," the animals snip off a bit of them until at last his ears are teeny tiny.

The Armadillo

The armadillo
As a pillow
Would really be swell
Except
For the fact
That it comes in a shell.

—by Douglas Florian

Rodeo Day (Movement, Art, Language Arts, and Math)

Invite students to round up some western gear and come to school dressed as a cowboy or cowgirl for Rodeo Day. Celebrate with one or more of the following events:

◎ **Horse Races:** Use cones to set up a course outdoors or in the gym in a figure 8, bow tie or letter W configuration. Challenge students to race from start to finish while riding a "hobbyhorse."

◎ **Fancy Boots:** Let each child design and decorate a boot. (Provide a cowboy boot pattern for them to trace, or let them draw their own.) Have children use catalog copy as a model for writing a description of their boots. Use the boots to create a catalog of boots, complete with descriptions.

◎ **Rodeo Talk:** Using a dictionary, let teams of students race to be the first to define these rodeo words: *brand, chaps, earmark,* and *stampede.*

◎ **Rope Tricks:** Cut a length of rope into several different-sized pieces (one per student). Place the rope in a bag and let each student choose a piece. Ask students to measure their rope. Have them organize their pieces of rope in different arrangements—for example, from shortest to longest or in concentric circles.

Word Study: Number Words (Language Arts and Math)

One of the most amazing things about armadillos is that the mother always gives birth to four identical babies. Use this fact to explore "number words" with students.

◎ Write "quadruplet" on the chalkboard. Explain that a quadruplet is one of four babies born at the same time. Challenge students to find and list words for other multiple births—for example, *twins* and *triplets.*

◎ Name and list other words that answer "how much" or "how many," such as *few, couple, ton, mile, yard, handful, pinch, smidgen.* Which ones reference specific amounts? Which ones reference estimates?

Rhyme Time (Language Arts, Science, and Art)

Many children have never seen an armadillo. Use this poem as a springboard to talk about its physical characteristics.

Ask children to describe what the author means when he says "it comes in a shell." Explain that armadillos are covered in armor, which consists of closely fitted plates of bone with hair growing between them. In fact, that is how they got their name—*armadillo* means "little armored one" in Spanish. Show students pictures of armadillos. Discuss the purpose of an armadillo's armor. Invite students to use recycled materials and art supplies such as egg cartons, clay, or bottle caps to create models of these armored creatures.

Dig Up Some Facts

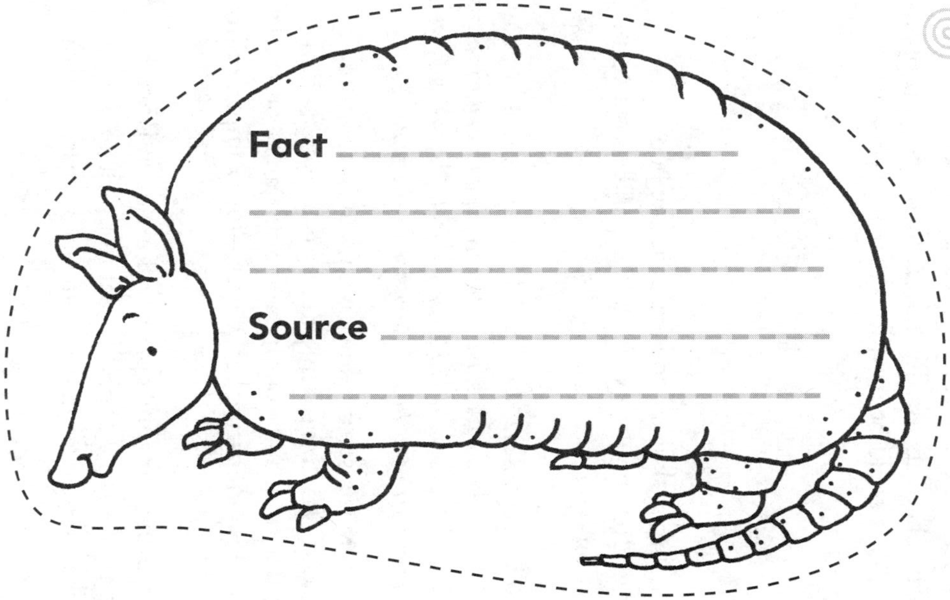

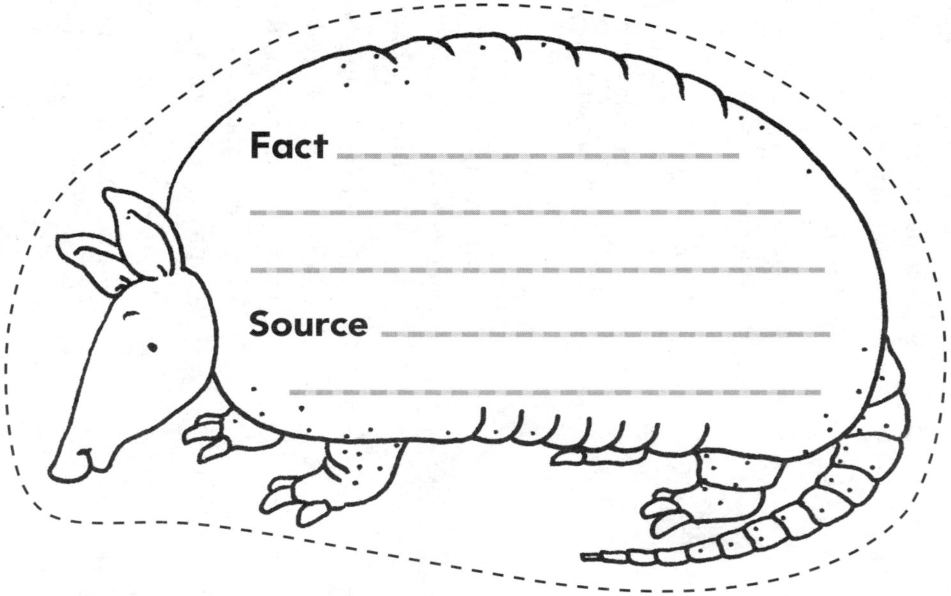

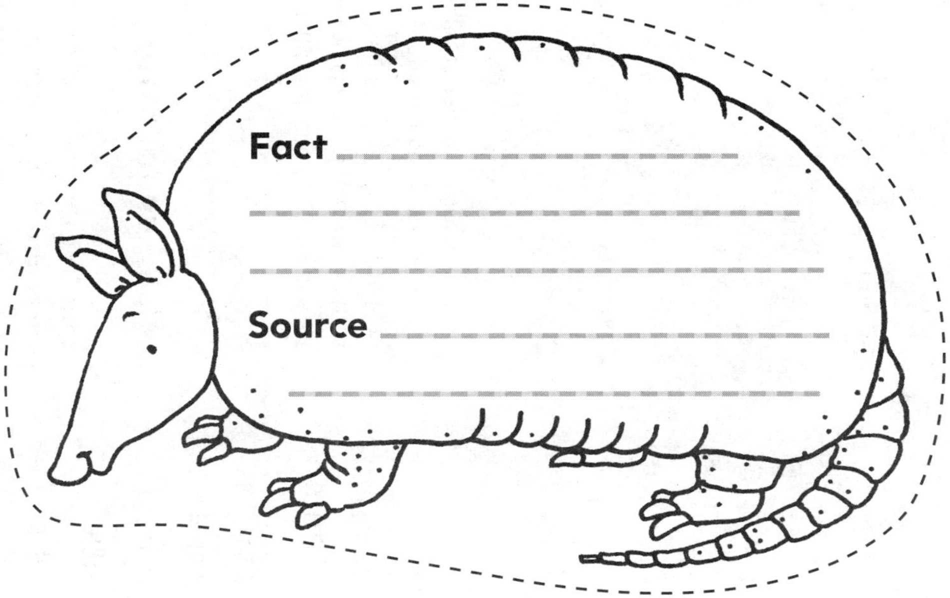

Fact _____

Source _____

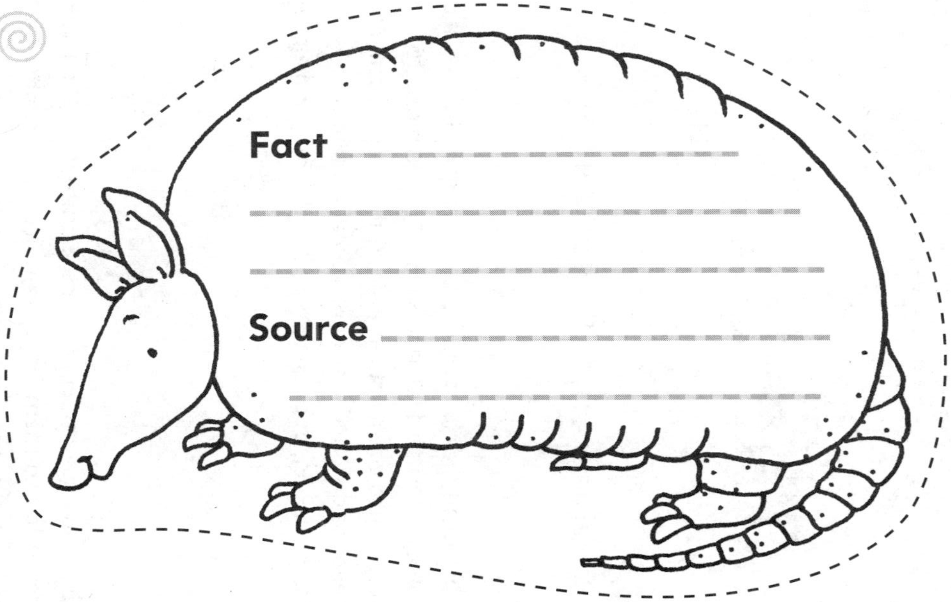

Fact _____

Source _____

Fact _____

Source _____

Fact _____

Source _____

The Hat

(G.P. PUTNAM'S SONS, 1997)

When Lisa's woolen stocking is blown off the clothesline, curious Hedgie discovers it and pokes his nose inside. It gets stuck on his prickles, and soon all the animals are laughing at his "stocking hat." To avoid embarrassment, he justifies the hat with comments such as "when it rains, my hat will keep me dry" and "my ears will be warm in a snowstorm." This gets the other animals thinking, and soon they all find "hats" of their own.

Concepts and Themes

▲▲▲▲▲▲▲

☼ animals

☼ clothing

☼ winter

☼ perspective

Before Reading

Mistaken Identity

Introduce the story with an activity in which students, like the animals in the book, try to identify an object that is unfamiliar to them. Find an object that is most likely unfamiliar to students—for example, an unusual kitchen tool or an antiquated gadget. Pass the object around and let students examine it closely. Ask students to give the object a name and speculate about its use. Reveal the identity of the object and its use. Is it possible that the object could be used for other purposes such as those suggested by students?

After Reading

Reinforce compare/contrast skills as you examine the book's similarity to other Jan Brett books, as well as the parallels between Lisa's winter preparations and our own.

◎ Read aloud or revisit *The Mitten* (page 22). Ask: "In what ways is this book like *The Hat*?" (*for example, each has a cumulative story structure; each involves animals and some item of clothing; each involves a child losing something*) "In what ways are they different?" (*for example, one is set on a farm, the other in the woods*)

◎ In many of Jan Brett's books, there is a second story going on in the borders. Ask students if they noticed what Lisa was doing while the animals were talking to Hedgie about his hat. Revisit the book and examine the oval frames on the left side of each spread. Most show Lisa preparing for winter—for example, filling a bird feeder and waxing skis.

◎ Ask students to name ways in which their family prepares for winter. Discuss whether the ways they prepare are the same as or different from what Lisa does. Ask: "Does where a person lives make a difference in how someone prepares for winter?"

Clothesline Math (Math)

Did students notice how the clothes began disappearing with each turn of the page? Use this detail of the book to introduce or reinforce subtraction skills.

◎ Revisit the book and draw students' attention to the top of each double-page spread. What do they notice about the clothesline? (*There are fewer clothes on each page.*) How did that happen? (*The wind blew the clothes away.*)

◎ Work together with students to write number sentences that show what happens in each picture of the clothesline.

◎ To create an interactive display, staple a length of rope to a bulletin board. Use clothespins to display hats, mittens, heavy socks, scarves, and other winter clothing. Write subtraction number sentences on index cards, place them in an envelope, and staple the envelope to the board.

◎ Let students take turns choosing a card and manipulating the clothing to match the number sentence.

All About Animals in Winter (Science and Language Arts)

The animals in the story found hats to keep them warm in the winter. How do animals really prepare for the cold season? Work together to create a nonfiction class book about animals and their winter habitats.

◎ Introduce students to the words *migration*, *hibernation*, and *dormancy*. Chart examples of animals that migrate, hibernate, and enter periods of dormancy. Also include a category for animals that remain active. Examples of each follow:

> **Migrate:** some birds, butterflies
> **Hibernate:** bats, woodchucks, bears
> **Enter Periods of Dormancy:** skunks, raccoons, chipmunks
> **Remain Active:** beaver, rabbits, squirrels, deer

◎ Discuss the winter habitats of the animals in *The Hat*. Find out about other animals, too.

◎ Let each student choose an animal and create a page for a book that names and pictures the animal, and tells what its winter habitat is and why. To go further, examine features of nonfiction books for children, such as a glossary and index, and work with children to include these in the class book.

Skunks sleep in burrows when it is cold. Their holes are lined with dry grass and leaves.

Tip

▲ ▲ ▲ ▲ ▲ ▲

Learn how animals prepare for winter with these Web sites:

Animals in Winter:
www.sciencemadesimple.com/animals.html

How Do Animals Adapt to Winter?
www.iwla.org/yikes/wl_animalwinter.html

Book Links

Animals Should Definitely Not Wear Clothing
by Judi Barrett
(Aladdin, 1989).

Children will enjoy the silly illustrations of a sheep wearing a wool sweater, a giraffe wearing neckties, and a chicken wearing pants—each in response to the question, "Why shouldn't animals wear clothing?"

Hats, Hats, Hats
by Ann Morris
(Mulberry Books, 1993).

This books celebrates the diversity of the world with dazzling photographs of hats, hats, and more hats!

Who Took the Farmer's Hat?
by Joan Nodset
(HarperTrophy, 1988).

When the wind takes the farmer's old brown hat, he questions the animals to see if they have seen it. Squirrel, Mouse, and Duck each reply, "No," but then describe something they have seen that bears a striking resemblance to his hat. Finally, when Bird shows him his "nice round brown nest," he realizes his hat has found a better purpose.

A Hat of One's Own (Art)

What was really a stocking became the animals' creative interpretation of a hat. Invite students to use their creativity to design and make hats of their own.

◎ Invite children to create a unique hat using found materials such as paper bags, newspaper, foil, or even bubble wrap. Students can decorate their hats using materials such as yarn, ribbon, and buttons.

◎ Let students show off their millinery creations by scheduling a hat parade or fashion show.

Word Study: Winter Word Bank (Language Arts)

Prepare for a season of writing by creating a winter word bank. Work together with students to brainstorm "winter words" such as *coats*, *cold*, and *skating*. Group the words into categories such as "Clothing" and "Weather." Record the words in each category on a hat-shaped chart. Encourage students to use the word bank as a resource while writing stories of their own.

Rhyme Time (Language Arts)

Students will have fun creating illustrations for a poem about hats.

◎ Give each student a copy of the poem (page 47) and read it aloud.

◎ Assign each student a different hat—for example, ski hat or hat with feathers. Have students draw and cut out a picture of the hat.

◎ Turn the poem into an illustrated book by writing each line on a different page and gluing students' pictures onto the pages accordingly. Add a cover and a title, and staple pages to bind.

Name _____ Date _____

Hats, Hats, Hats

One hat, two hats
Peekaboo hats

Old hats, new hats
See right through hats

Soft, fuzzy, furry hats
Swish, in a hurry hats

Yard hats, hard hats
Hats that flap

Ski hats, tree hats
Hats that snap

Hats with tassles
Hats with feathers

Hats to wear
In rainy weather

Hats for cold
Hats for shade

Hats in stores
And hats homemade

Hats in closets
Hats on beds

Match up hats
They all need heads.

—by Nancy White Carlstrom

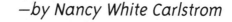

Gingerbread Baby

(G.P. PUTNAM'S SONS, 1999)

Concepts and Themes

▲ ▲ ▲ ▲ ▲ ▲

☼ problem solving

☼ folktales

☼ cooking

☼ winter holidays

☼ senses

Tip

▲ ▲ ▲ ▲ ▲ ▲

To learn about the origins of gingerbread and to view some unusual gingerbread houses, including a castle, check these Web sites:

The History of Gingerbread:

WW Wiz Magazine:
wwwiz/issue04/wiz%5fd04.html

Gingerbread Sculpture:

C. B. Hannegans:
cbhannegans.com/gingerbread
.html

Following a recipe found in an old cookbook, Matti and his mom make a gingerbread boy and place him in the oven. The directions say "Do not peek," but Matti finds it difficult to wait. Much to his surprise, when he opens the oven door, out jumps a gingerbread baby! Who will catch him? In the end it's Matti's clever plan that puts an end to the chase.

Before Reading

Revisit the Folktale

. . . .

Read aloud several versions of the folktale that inspired *Gingerbread Baby* (see Related Resources). Create a chart with students to compare the beginning, middle, and ending of the stories. Ask: "Which part of the story showed the most variation between versions (beginning, middle, or end)? Which beginning did you like best? Middle? End?"

A New Ending

. . . .

As you introduce *Gingerbread Baby*, and before reading it, share with students that when Jan Brett was a little girl and heard the story of the *Gingerbread Boy*, she wanted to "jump into the book and save him from being eaten up by the crafty fox" (from Newsnotes on **www.janbrett.com**). So when she decided to illustrate the story, she created a new ending where the gingerbread boy doesn't get eaten. Let students have some fun with their own *Gingerbread Baby* endings.

The gingerbread boy growled very loud and he scared the fox away!

◎ Give each student a gingerbread cutout. (page 52)

◎ Invite students to use the cutout to record their predictions for the ending of *Gingerbread Baby*. Encourage them to think like the author. Ask: "How will the story end so that the gingerbread boy (baby) doesn't get eaten?"

◎ Let students take turns sharing their ideas. Then read the story to find out the author's ending.

After Reading

 Use the story to explore story structure as well as what beginnings, middles, and endings sometimes have in common.

◎ Once you've shared the story, record its beginning, middle, and ending on the chart. (See Before Reading, Revisit the Folktale, page 48.) Ask: "How is this version similar to the other versions we read? Different from the other versions?"

◎ Let students compare their predictions with the ending of the story. How are their endings alike? How are they different? What else did Jan Brett do to make her story original? (This is an opportunity to explore characters and setting.)

Extension Activities

Dear Matti (Language Arts and Social Studies)

The character of Matti empowers children because he uses his creativity to solve a problem that the other characters (including many adults) weren't able to solve. On her Web site the author notes, "Matti was inspired by a real little boy named Alexander who is also creative and always looks as if he has a plan." Sharpen students' problem-solving skills, and their ability to understand character, with an activity that lets them write and respond to a letter.

◎ Introduce letter-writing as a form of writing. Ask students what they know about writing letters. Review parts of a letter and various reasons people write letters.

◎ Have students write a "Dear Matti" letter that tells of a problem they are having. To reinforce writing skills, encourage students to include details in their letter-writing.

◎ Have students exchange papers and respond to the letter with one or more suggestions or solutions to the problem. Again, to reinforce the use of details in writing, ask students to clearly explain their solutions.

◎ Follow up with a discussion that reinforces the idea that although we can often solve problems on our own, it is sometimes helpful to seek the advice of others.

Create a Class Shield (Social Studies)

Explore the author's use of borders as a way of telling part of the story.

◎ Challenge students to find the page in the book that displays colorful shields in the border. These represent the 25 *cantons*, or districts, of Switzerland.

◎ Using the shield shapes in the book as models, have students create a shield to represent their classroom community. Encourage them to choose colors that are meaningful (such as school colors) and include symbols that illustrate the class rules, goals, agreements, or accomplishments. Display the shields to remind students of the community they share.

Tip

▲▲▲▲▲

As with *Gingerbread Baby*, many books follow a problem-solution story structure. Choose one and read it aloud. Stop before the conclusion. Let children share ways they would solve the character's problem.

To make gingerbread cookies, use the recipe at www.janbrett.com or use refrigerated cookie dough.

The Sweet Shop (Math)

Sharpen students' consumer skills by setting up a "sweet shop" where they can purchase items to decorate gingerbread cookies.

◎ Send home a note requesting that each student bring to school one item that can be used to decorate gingerbread, such as candy, raisins, or frosting. Place each item in a separate covered container and attach a price tag—for example, 1 cent each or 25 cents.

◎ Give each student a paper bag and the same amount of money (play or real).

◎ Invite students to visit the Sweet Shop, make their purchases, and use the items to decorate a gingerbread man or house.

Word Study: Silly Compound Cookbook (Language Arts)

Build word analysis skills by using the title of the book as a springboard for a lesson on compound words.

◎ Draw students' attention to the word *gingerbread* on the cover of the book. Invite students to tell what they think this kind of word is called.

◎ Explain that *gingerbread* is a compound word, which is created by putting two words together. Let students identify the two words (*ginger* and *bread*).

◎ Challenge students to identify other foods that are also compound words—for example, *gumdrop, meatloaf,* and *oatmeal.* Write the words that make up each compound word on a separate index card—for example, *ginger, bread, gum, drop, meat, loaf, oat,* and *meal.*

◎ Have students put their words together to make a new compound word, write it at the top of a sheet of paper, and illustrate the "dish."

◎ Compile the pages into a book and label it "Silly Compound Cookbook." To go further, students can create a recipe for their dish, complete with an ingredient list and set of directions.

The Smell Test (Science)

Most would agree that the smell of gingerbread baking in the oven is delightful! Challenge students to explore their sense of smell as they investigate the question, "Do all things have an odor?"

◎ Copy the record sheet on page 53. Gather the ingredients listed to make gingerbread. Place them at a center. Give each student a record sheet.

◎ Let students take turns "sniffing" each item. Show them how to color in the gingerbread ("yes" or "no") for each ingredient to answer the question, "Can you smell it?"

◎ Invite students to compare their results. Which ingredients could they all smell? Were there ingredients that some, but not all, could smell?

◎ Explain that the ability to detect odors varies from person to person. This may be due to genetics, injury, or blocked nasal passages that occur when someone has a cold or allergies. There were probably some ingredients that no one was able to smell, such as salt and baking soda. These would be considered odorless because our sense of smell is unable to detect them. Challenge students to name other substances they consider odorless. To go further, let students set up investigations to test their ideas. (Check substances first for safety.)

Rhyme Time (Language Arts)

A variation of a familiar rhyme invites children to practice letter recognition and sound-spelling relationships beginning with words they know best—their names!

◎ Teach students the following rhyme. Fill in the blank with students' names:

> Pat-a-cake, pat-a-cake, baker's man,
> Bake me some gingerbread as fast as you can;
> Roll it and pat it and mark it with a *G*,
> Put it in the oven for _____ and me.

◎ Copy the rhyme onto sentence strips. Glue the strips to posterboard and laminate.

◎ Create strips with students' names. Attach Velcro to the blank space on the chart and onto the back of each name card.

◎ Let students select a name to fill in the blank and then practice reading the chart aloud.

Let students create scratch-and-sniff gingerbread men by cutting gingerbread shapes from sandpaper and rubbing them with cinnamon sticks.

Book Links

The Gingerbread Boy
by Richard Egielski
(HarperCollins, 2000).

This version of the tale finds the gingerbread boy in an urban setting, where he is chased by a rat, some construction workers, a policeman, and others.

The Gingerbread Man
by Jim Aylesworth
(Scholastic, 1998).

The illustrations found in this traditional version are seemingly old-fashioned and resemble early editions of Mother Goose.

The Gingerbread Man
by Eric Kimmel
(Holiday House, 1994).

This classic retelling ends on an upbeat note as it suggests that gingerbread men return whenever someone bakes gingerbread.

Gingerbread Pattern

Teaching With Favorite Jan Brett Books   Scholastic Teaching Resources

The Smell Test

Ingredient	Yes	No
flour		
salt		
baking soda		
ginger		
cinnamon		
cloves		
nutmeg		
butter		
brown sugar		
egg		
molasses		
vanilla		

Hedgie's Surprise

(G.P. PUTNAM'S SONS, 2000)

Concepts and Themes

* friendship
* life cycles
* eggs
* trickster tales

Poor Henny! She longs to have a family just like Goosey-Goosey, but each day her eggs are stolen by a mischievous Tomten. Unsure what to do, she consults with her wise friend Hedgie, who devises a clever plan to trick the Tomten and teach him a good lesson.

Before Reading

Surprise!

Show students the cover of the book and read aloud the title. Explain that the story is about two friends named Henny and Hedgie. Henny is bothered by a Tomten who keeps stealing her eggs from her nest. One day Hedgie tries to stop the Tomten by giving him a "surprise." Can students predict the "surprise" suggested in the title, or will the book have a true surprise ending? Give each student a plastic egg. Ask students to write down what they predict Hedgie's surprise will be and place it in the egg. After reading the story, let students exchange eggs and read each other's predictions aloud. Did the ending surprise everyone?

After Reading

Students will no doubt be amused by the mischievous Tomten and the tricks Henny and Hedgie played on him. Use this aspect of the story to introduce the genre of trickster tales.

◎ Ask students to name other stories that contain "tricksters," as in *Hedgie's Surprise*. Explain that these are often called trickster tales.

◎ If possible, read several trickster tales aloud to the class. Examples include *Anansi the Spider: A Tale From the Ashanti*, by Gerald McDermott (Henry Holt, 1987); *Coyote: A Trickster Tale From the American Southwest*, by Gerald McDermott (Voyager Books, 1999); and *The Tale of the Tricky Fox*, by Jim Aylesworth (Scholastic, 2001). Discuss the different ways in which characters in the stories play a trick on others.

Tip

This is a good opportunity for a writing connection. Students can write trickster tales starring themselves!

◎ Make connections between the story and students' experiences by inviting them to tell about times they've played tricks on someone. Ask: "When is it okay to play a trick on someone? When is it not okay?"

Extension Activities

Tomten Tricks From A to Z (Language Arts)

Make an alphabet book to extend the story and help students imagine other objects that could have been used to trick the Tomten.

◎ Write the following text from the book on sentence strips and place them in a pocket chart:

> "'Henny! Have you got a little yummy for my nearly empty tummy?'
> The Tomten reached for an egg and pulled out a(n)
> _____ .'"

◎ Read the sentences aloud with students. Work together to create picture and word cards for the following objects: acorn, strawberry, mushroom, potato. Let children take turns placing the picture and word cards in the blank and rereading the text.

◎ As an extension of the story, assign each student a letter of the alphabet. Ask children to think of an object starting with that letter that might trick the Tomten. Have children copy the text from the pocket chart, fill in the blank with the name for their object, and draw a picture.

◎ Give children sheets of paper sized to cover their alphabet objects. Have children glue the top edge of the paper to the picture so that it covers the drawing of their object and creates a flap. To complete the page, on the flap have children draw a picture of Henny sitting on her nest.

◎ Place the pages in alphabetical order, add a cover, and staple. Share the book with students, and let them take turns sharing it at home, along with a copy of *Hedgie's Surprise*.

Breakfast Graph (Math)

The Tomten likes to eat porridge and eggs for breakfast. Ask students: "What do you like to eat for breakfast?" Guide students in conducting a survey to find out. Display results of the survey on the chalkboard in the form of a table. Review ways of graphing data. Then let each student create a graph based on the information collected. Discuss the graph, asking:

⁂ "How many different breakfast foods are preferred by students in our class? Are these results surprising? Why?"

⁂ "What was the most popular breakfast food? Least?"

⁂ "How many students like eggs, like the Tomten?"

⁂ "Who would find this information useful? How?"

⁂ "What doesn't this graph tell us?"

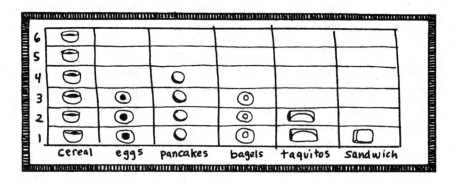

Word Study: Whose Is It? (Language Arts)

The Tomten doesn't seem to understand what belongs to him and what doesn't! Use this theme from the story to teach about possessives.

◎ Write the following on the chalkboard:

Hedgie	goslings
Tomten	eggs
Henny	prickles
Goosey-Goosey	porridge

◎ Ask children to match the objects to their owners.

◎ Model how to use apostrophes to show possessives. Let students try themselves by writing the characters' names and their belongings in possessive form—for example, "Hedgie's prickles."

◎ For practice, invite students to create more examples of possessives based on the book. Have them write the two parts to the possessive on different cards. Combine the cards for a class-made matching game that reinforces this writing skill.

Eggs-periment (Science)

How were Henny's chicks able to breathe while inside their eggs? Conduct this experiment to find out.

◎ Place a raw egg (in the shell) in a clear jar half-filled with warm water.

◎ Guide students to discover the bubbles coming from the egg.

◎ Have students use words and pictures to record their observations.

◎ Ask: "What does this tell us about eggs?" (*The eggshell is porous— it has holes in it so that air can go in and out of the egg. The bubbles children see are air bubbles.*) Ask: "What does this tell us about chicks?" (*The growing chicks receive air through the holes in the egg.*)

Rhyme Time (Math and Language Arts)

Share a number rhyme to help children learn doubles math facts (through 10 + 10).

> Five eggs and five eggs, that makes ten.
> Sitting on top is a mother hen.
> Crackle, crackle, crackle,
> What do you see?
> Ten yellow chicks, fluffy as can be.

◎ Ask students to write a number sentence to illustrate the number of eggs in the poem (for example, 5 + 5 = 10). Explain that this number sentence is called a double because the two addends are the same.

◎ Make a Doubles Math Facts book for each student. Use the sample (right) as a pattern. Make 10 copies for each book. Add a cover page that reads "I'm Seeing Double" or "Count Your Chickens Before They Hatch." Staple the pages together.

◎ Let students complete a page for each of the doubles (for example, 1 + 1, 2 + 2, and 3 + 3) by writing the number sentence in the space provided and drawing the corresponding eggs in each nest.

◎ Encourage students to use the books to help them memorize all the doubles facts.

Book Links

Eggs: A Photographic Story of Hatching
by Robert Burton
(DK Publishing, 1994).

Use this book to explore the life cycles of several different animals that lay eggs.

The Tomten
by Astrid Lindgren
(Penguin Putnam, 1997).

This magical story, based on a poem, invites you to follow the Tomten around the farm as he tiptoes on small, silent feet through winter darkness. He speaks to all the animals in Tomten language—a language only they can understand.

Doubles Math Facts

O + O = O

+ =

_____ _____ _____

Daisy Comes
Home

(G.P. PUTNAM'S SONS, 2002)

When Daisy, the smallest of Mei Mei's hens, is picked on by the other hens, she decides to sleep outside in a market basket. While she rests, the river creeps up from behind and carries her on an adventure where she learns some useful survival skills.

Concepts and Themes

- ☼ survival
- ☼ China
- ☼ friendship
- ☼ hens

Before Reading

Guess the Title

Jan Brett had a difficult time deciding what to name this story. In addition to *Daisy Comes Home*, she considered *Happy Hens* and *Fine Feathered Friends* (source: **www.janbrett.com**). Use sticky notes to cover up the title. Show the book to students and share the three titles. Once you have read the book aloud, ask them to name the title they think is best and tell why. Remove the sticky notes and reveal the actual title. Let students tell why they think the author chose this one of the three she considered. Let students share their own ideas for other titles that work well for this story.

After Reading

Strengthen inferential thinking with a discussion about lost and found objects. Use the following questions to invite students' ideas:

- ◎ "The fisherman in the story assumed he could keep Daisy because he found her. Was he correct? What would you have done?"

- ◎ "Have you ever lost or found something? What steps did you take to retrieve the object or return it to its owner?'

- ◎ "What does the saying 'Finders keepers, losers weepers' mean? How do you feel about this saying?"

Story Map Journeys

(Language Arts and Social Studies)

In the story, Daisy takes an unexpected journey. Explore story structure by inviting students to create a map of her travels.

◎ On a sheet of paper, list the different places she went and the people and animals she encountered.

◎ Have students draw pictures for each of these people, places, and animals.

◎ Create puppets for Mei Mei and Daisy by attaching their pictures to craft sticks.

◎ Arrange the remaining pictures on a sheet of mural paper in the order they first appear in the story, and glue them in place.

◎ Let students take turns using the puppets and mural to retell the story of *Daisy Comes Home*.

Let's Compare Journeys! (Language Arts)

The Story About Ping, by Marjorie Flack (Viking, 1977), tells of another character who finds himself on a journey, and like *Daisy Comes Home*, it also takes place in China. Jan Brett remembers listening to this story when she was a little girl. Use a Venn diagram to compare the two stories.

◎ To create the diagram, draw two intersecting circles on the chalkboard or on a sheet of posterboard.

◎ Write a book title in each circle.

◎ Compare the books. Record the ways the books are different in the two separate circles and the ways they are the same in the space where the circles intersect.

◎ Can students think of other stories in which the character takes a journey? Create new Venn diagrams to make more comparisons.

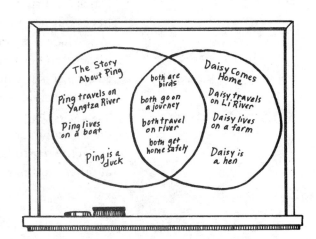

Book Links

Count Your Way Through China
by Jim Haskins
(Carolrhoda Books, 1988).

This book introduces children to the geography and culture of China while teaching them to count to ten in Chinese.

Hilda Hen's Scary Night
by Mary Wormell
(Harcourt, 1997).

Hilda is late getting back to her henhouse. In the dark, she is startled by many "creatures" that turn out to be farmyard objects that look much spookier at night.

Word Study: Two Sounds of Y (Language Arts)

This activity will help children understand the phrase "A-E-I-O-U and sometimes Y."

◎ Write the name "Daisy" on the chalkboard.

◎ Ask: "What sound does the letter *y* make at the end of the word?" (long *e*) "Can you think of other names that end with this sound?" Explain that *y* sometimes acts as a vowel when it has the sound of a long *e* or long *i*.

◎ Cut out several eggs from construction paper. Place them in a box.

◎ As students read, encourage them to record on the egg cutouts words that represent the two sounds of *y*.

◎ Sort the words by the two sounds and read them aloud together.

Rhyme Time

Many students have heard "Sticks and stones may break my bones but names will never hurt me." Share a poem to help students understand that this adage just isn't true. As a follow-up, invite children to create posters of the poem to display in the classroom and around school as a reminder to be considerate of others' feelings.

Don't Say "Crybaby!"

Don't say "Crybaby!"
Don't say "Dummy!"
Teasing makes me
Feel so crummy.

Falling down
Can bruise my knees,
But words can hurt
Where no one sees.

—by Judy Lalli

Teaching With Other Favorite Jan Brett Books

The First Dog

(HARCOURT BRACE, 1988)

A cave boy befriends a Paleowolf when he exchanges rhino ribs for protection from dangerous beasts of the Ice Age.

Fast-Forward Rewrite

Explore the prehistoric period in which the story took place. Show children a time line to give them a sense of how far back in history this story goes. How would the story be different if it was rewritten to take place during present time? What food would Kip have with him that the dog would have wanted? What dangers might the boy encounter on his adventures? How would the dog protect him? Work together with children to write a similar tale set in modern times about the adventures of a boy and his dog.

Poetry for the Senses

Revisit the book and draw students' attention to the keen senses of the Paleowolf. What did the wolf smell? What did he hear? What did he see? If possible, take children outdoors and let them use their own senses to explore their surroundings. Have them write descriptive phrases that tell what they smell, hear, and see.

Happy Birthday, Dear Duck

by Eve Bunting, illustrated by Jan Brett

(CLARION BOOKS, 1988)

In a suspenseful story set in the desert, Duck gets birthday presents that are better suited for the beach. Duck is puzzled until Turtle finally arrives with the last gift—a plastic pool!

A Desert Birthday

Use the following questions to guide a discussion that explores how the setting of a story relates to the plot:

* "How important is the desert setting to this story?"
* "Could this story work in other settings?"
* "Why is a pool a good gift for a story that takes place in the desert?"
* "What gifts might Duck receive if the story took place near a lake or ocean?"
* "Do the animals in the book live in the desert? If not, where do you think they live?"

The Mystery Gift

The suspense builds in the story as Duck is about to open his last gift. What could it be? Stop reading and ask children to wonder about this last gift. Have them name the other gifts he received. What do they have in common? How do they think this next gift will relate to the others? Let each child record a prediction on a present-shaped cutout. Continue reading, and let children check their predictions.

Beauty and the Beast

(CLARION BOOKS, 1989)

Beauty's father becomes indebted to the Beast when he picks a rose from the Beast's garden. In exchange for her father's life, Beauty agrees to move into the palace with the Beast, where she soon discovers that appearances can be deceiving.

Shadow Art

Revisit the book and draw children's attention to the shadow paintings found in the background of some pages. Use these questions to explore how the illustrations help tell this story:

✳ "What do these paintings show?"

✳ "Why do you think Jan Brett included them in the book?"

✳ "What do the sayings above the paintings mean? How are they messages to Beauty?"

✳ "How do the paintings and messages provide clues to the reader?"

Judging a Book by Its Cover

Explore the theme of the story and the expression "You can't judge a book by its cover," using the following exercise:

✳ Cut out a picture of a person from a magazine. Share it with children. Ask: "What can you tell me about this person?" Record students' responses and then sort them by categories: "On the Outside" and "On the Inside."

✳ Discuss results of the sorting. Invite students to tell how this relates to the theme of the story and to the expression "You can't judge a book by its cover."

The Owl and the Pussycat

(G.P. PUTNAM'S SONS, 1991)

Introduce nonsense poetry with this classic by Edward Lear about two unlikely sweethearts who travel through the Caribbean on a pea green boat in search of wedded bliss.

What's a Runcible Spoon?

Some of the vocabulary used in this book may be unfamiliar to students. Play this game to help them learn the definitions. Divide the class into two teams, the "owls" and the "pussycats." Give each student a dictionary. Write a word from the story on the chalkboard. Let students race to be the first one to score a point for his or her team by reading aloud the dictionary definition. The team with the most points at the end of the game wins.

Nonsense Poetry

Use this book as an introduction to Edward Lear's poetry. Ask: "Why is it considered nonsense poetry? What elements make it so? Are there other poets you know who also write nonsense poetry?" (for example, Lewis Carroll) Compare and contrast various examples and then invite children to write their own nonsense poems.

Comet's Nine Lives

(G.P. Putnam's Sons, 1996)

As a roaming feline searches for a permanent home, his nine lives slowly diminish when he comes face to face with danger.

Story Map

Invite children to chart Comet's journey around Nantucket Island by creating a story map. Begin by listing all the places Comet visited and then sequencing them according to the order they appear in the book. Next, have children draw the island on a sheet of paper and create pictures to represent each stop he made. Children can then connect the stops using dotted lines or arrows. Help children label the map and record each of Comet's nine lives.

Step Books

Use the format of a step book to sequence the events of *Comet's Nine Lives*. To create the book, give each child five sheets of paper. Demonstrate how to stagger the bottom of each. Next, have them fold the top down, creating 10 steps. Staple at the top. On the first step, have children write the title of the story. Label the succeeding nine steps 1 through 9. Under each flap, have children draw a picture and write a sentence that tells how each life was lost. For nine, children can depict Comet's happy new home.

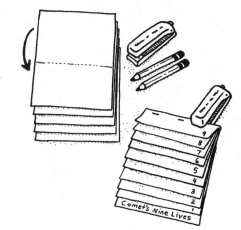

On Noah's Ark

(G.P. Putnam's Sons, 2003)

Noah's granddaughter keeps the peace on a crowded ark as the animals become restless and tangled during their 40-day-40-night voyage.

Two by Two

The two-by-two formation by which the animals boarded the ark serves as a great introduction to multiplication. Using pairs of toy animals, let children solve problems based on the twos times table—for example, "If there are five pairs of animals, how many animals are on the ark all together? How many pairs are on the ark if there are 20 animals all together?"

Move Like the Animals

The story uses descriptive language to tell how the animals move. On slips of paper, write different animal names. Let each child choose a slip and record an adjective that tells how that animal might move. For example, "the leopard leaped." Place the slips in a bag and let children take turns choosing one. Invite them to act out the animal and its movement for classmates to guess.

The Umbrella

(G.P. Putnam's Sons, 2004)

Carlos heads to the cloud forest with his tropical umbrella in search of animals. When he climbs a tree for a better view, the animals find his umbrella and use it as a resting place.

Umbrella Reports

This book includes some animals that may be unfamiliar to children, such as the kinkajou, tapir, and quetzal. Divide the class into small groups and assign each group an animal from the book. (Clip art of each animal is available at **www.janbrett.com**.) Ask children to research their animal and organize findings using an "umbrella organizer" containing several different spokes, one for each category of information.

El Paraguas (The Umbrella)

Throughout this book, Jan Brett introduces children to several Spanish words and phrases, such as *buena suerte* and *no problema*. Challenge children to figure out what the words mean by using the context of the sentence. Consult an English-Spanish dictionary to check for accuracy.